Table of Contents

INTRODUCTION

The term negotiation refers to a strategic discussion intended to resolve an issue in a way that both parties find acceptable. Negotiations involve give and take, which means one or both parties will usually need to make some concessions. Negotiation can take place between buyers and sellers, employers and prospective employees, two or more governments, and other parties. Here is how negotiation works and advice for negotiating successfully.

HOW NEGOTIATIONS WORK

Negotiations involve two or more parties who come together to reach some end goal that is agreeable to all those involved. One party will put its position forward, while the other will either accept the conditions presented or counter with its own position. The process continues until both parties agree to a resolution or negotiations break off without one. Experienced negotiators will often try to learn as much as possible about the other party's position before a negotiation begins, including what the strengths and weaknesses of that position are, how to prepare to defend their positions, and any counter-arguments the other party will likely make.

The length of time it takes for negotiations to conclude depends on the circumstances. Negotiation can take as little as a few minutes, or, in more complex cases, much longer. For example, a buyer and seller may negotiate for minutes or hours for the sale of a car. But the governments of two or more countries may take months or years to negotiate the terms of a major trade deal. Some negotiations require the use of a skilled negotiator such as a professional advocate, a real estate agent or broker, or an attorney.

Examples of Negotiations

Negotiating can take place between individuals, businesses, governments, and in any other situation where two parties have competing interests. Here are two everyday examples:

Say you plan to buy a new SUV but don't want to pay the full manufacturer's suggested retail price (MSRP). In that case, you might offer what you consider a fair price. The dealer can accept your offer or counter with another price figure. If you have good negotiating skills, you may be able to drive the price down to a level where you're happy and the dealer is still able to walk away with a profit, albeit a slimmer one.

Or, suppose you've been offered a new job but don't consider the salary sufficient. An employer's first compensation offer is often not its best possible offer, so it

may have some room to negotiate. In fact, a 2016 survey by the CareerBuilder website found that 73% of employers were open to negotiating a starting salary with job seekers. And if higher pay isn't a possibility, the employer may be willing to offer something additional, such as more vacation time or better benefits. In both of these examples—as in most successful negotiations—both parties have made compromises, while also achieving their principal goals. A 2022 study by Fidelity Investments found that while 58% of workers had accepted their employer's initial offer, 85% of those who attempted to negotiate got at least some of what they asked for.

The Stages of the Negotiation Process

Regardless of what you're negotiating over or with whom, negotiation usually involves several distinct steps.

Preparation

Before negotiations begin, there are a few questions it helps to ask yourself. Those include:

What do you hope to gain, ideally?

What are your realistic expectations?

What compromises are you willing to make?

What happens if you don't reach your end goal?

Preparation can also include finding out as much as you can about the other party and their likely point of view. In the case of the SUV negotiation above, you could probably find out how much room the dealer has to bargain by looking up actual sales prices for that vehicle online. Also, marshal any facts that will help you make a persuasive case. If you're negotiating for a new job or a raise at work, for instance, come armed with concrete examples of your accomplishments, including hard numbers if possible. Consider bringing testimonials from satisfied clients and/or coworkers if that will buttress your case. Many experienced negotiators consider preparation to be the single most important step in the entire process.

Exchanging Information

Once you're prepped for the negotiation, you're ready to sit down with the other party. If they're smart, they have probably prepared themselves, as well. This is the point at which both sides will present their initial positions in terms of what they want and are willing to give in return. Being able to clearly articulate your wishes is critical to the negotiation process. You may not get everything on your wish list, but the other party, if they want to reach a deal, will have a better idea of what it might take to make that happen. You will have a better idea of their position, and where they might be willing to bend, as well.

Bargaining

Now that both parties have laid out their case, you're ready to start bargaining. An important key to this step is to hear the other party out and refrain from being dismissive or argumentative. Successful negotiating involves a little give and take on both sides, and an adversarial relationship is likely to be less effective than a collegial one. Also bear in mind that a negotiation can take time, so try not to rush the process or allow yourself to be rushed.

Closing the Deal

Once both parties are satisfied with the results, it's time to end the negotiations. The next step may be in the form of a verbal agreement or written contract. The latter is usually a better idea as it clearly outlines the position of each party and can be enforced if one party doesn't live up to their end of the bargain.

Tips for Successful Negotiating

Some people may be born negotiators, but many of us are not. Here are a few tips that can help.

Justify Your Position. Don't just walk into negotiations without being able to back up your position. Bring information to show that you've done your research and you're committed to reaching a deal.

Put Yourself in Their Shoes. Remember that the other side has things it wants out of the deal, too. What can you offer that will help them reach their goal (or most of it) without giving away more than you want to or can afford to?

Keep Your Emotions in Check. It's easy to get caught up in the moment and be swayed by your personal feelings, especially ones like anger and frustration. But don't let your emotions cause you to lose sight of your goal.

Know When to Walk Away. Before you begin the negotiating process, it's a good idea to know what you'll accept as a bare minimum and when you'd rather walk away from the table than continue to bargain. There is no use trying to reach a deal if both sides are hopelessly dug in. Even if you don't want to end negotiations entirely, pausing them can give everyone involved a chance to regroup and possibly return to the table with a fresh perspective.

What Makes a Good Negotiator?
Some of the key skills of a good negotiator are the ability to listen, to think under pressure, to clearly articulate their point of view, and to be willing to compromise, within reason.

What Is ZOPA?

ZOPA is an acronym from the business world. It stands for zone of possible agreement. ZOPA is a way of visualizing where the positions of the parties to a negotiation overlap. It is within that zone that compromises can be reached.

What Is BATNA?

BATNA is another acronym from the world of business, meaning best alternative to a negotiated agreement. It refers to the next course of action a negotiator may take if a negotiation fails to arrive at a satisfactory conclusion. Veteran negotiators often go into a negotiation knowing what their likely BATNA would be, just in case.

HOW TO MASTER THE ART OF NEGOTIATION

Many people believe that negotiations are "all or nothing," and that there has to be one winner and one loser. Nothing could be further from the truth. While the goal of negotiation is most certainly getting what you want, the fact is that the best deals (the ones that stick) incorporate terms and ideas from both parties.

Before the Negotiation

Before entering any formal negotiation, it is important for an individual to think about what they want to achieve from the process. To that end, it makes sense to put on paper specific goals or desirable outcomes. Be optimistic. Ask yourself what would be a "home run" in your deal? This could be as simple as the other party conceding entirely to your wishes. Next, individuals should identify several fall-back positions that they'd be comfortable with that would still get the deal done. The idea is to have thought out as many scenarios as possible. The next task should be to identify (or try to identify) any potential weaknesses in the opposing party's position. For example, if in a real estate transaction, one party knows that the other party has to sell a certain property or face a liquidity crisis, this is valuable information that can be used in negotiation. Identification of weaknesses is important. That's because it might allow the party that has done its homework to capitalize on the other party's weaknesses and turn negotiations in its favor. At the very least, help both parties to identify an area of middle ground better.

Another pre-negotiation exercise — and it is something that most people don't do but should — is to come up with a list of reasons why their proposal would also be beneficial to the opposing party. The logic is to bring up the key points of this list in the actual negotiation with the counterparty in the hope that the points will advance the cause and/or help to identify some common ground. Again, using real estate as an example, perhaps one party (in this case a company) could argue that its bid for a particular property is more favorable than others (even though it's lower in terms of dollars) because it is an all-cash offer, as opposed to a riskier financing or a stock swap. By explicitly pointing out the advantages to both parties, the negotiator increases the odds of getting the deal done.

The Negotiation
In-Person

Ideally, each party should identify its goals and objectives at the outset. This allows each participant in the negotiation to know where the other stands. It also establishes a basis for a give-and-take conversation. At this point, each party may offer its fall-back proposals and counter-proposals to hammer out a deal. That said, beyond the initial back-and-forth of proposals, there are also other things that negotiators can do to enhance their chances of turning the deal in their favor. Let's use body language analysis as an example.

Was your proposal well received? Positive signs include nodding of the head and direct eye contact. Negative signs include folding of the arms (across the chest), aversion of eye contact, or a subtle head shake as if to say "no." Pay attention next time you ask someone a question. You'll see that more often than not, a person's body language can yield a lot of information regarding their underlying feelings.

By Phone

If negotiation is done over the phone, body language can't be determined. This means that the negotiator must do his best to analyze his counterpart's voice. As a general rule, extended pauses usually mean that the opposing party is hesitant or is pondering the offer. However, sudden exclamations or an unusually quick response (in a pleasant voice) may indicate that the opposing party is quite favorable to the proposal and needs a little nudge to seal the deal.

By E-Mail or Mail

Negotiations done through e-mail or the mail (such as residential real estate transactions) are a different animal altogether.

Here are some tips:

Words or phrases that leave ambiguity may signal that a party is open to a given proposal. Look specifically for words such as "can,""possibly,""perhaps,""maybe," or "acceptable." Also, if the party uses a phrase such as "anxiously awaiting your reply" or "looking forward to it," this may be a signal that the party is enthusiastic and/or optimistic that an agreement may soon be reached.

When the opposing party makes an initial offer or a counter-proposal, see if you can incorporate some of those ideas with your own and then seal the deal on the spot. If compromise on a particular issue is not possible, propose other alternatives that you think would be favorable to both parties.

Finally, a more formal contract reflecting the terms agreed upon during the negotiation is a must. To that end, have an attorney draft a formal contract soon after the negotiation process is completed and make certain that all parties sign it on time.

No Agreement? No Worries

If an agreement cannot be reached in one sitting or one phone call, leave the door open to future negotiations. If possible, schedule further meetings. Don't worry, if worded your request appropriately won't appear overly anxious. To the contrary, it will come across as though you sincerely believe that a deal can be worked out and that you are willing to work to make that happen. In between negotiations, try to review what took place during the initial meeting mentally. Did the opposing party reveal any weaknesses? Did they imply that other factors may have an impact on the deal? Pondering these questions before the next meeting can give the negotiator a leg up on their counterpart.

Not every negotiation can reach a deal that all sides are happy with. Whatever happens, f an agreement can't be reached, agree to part as friends. Never, under any circumstances, burn your bridges. You never know when you might have to cross those rivers again.

Liquidity Crisis: A Lack of Short Term Cash Flow

A liquidity crisis is a financial situation characterized by a lack of cash or easily-convertible-to-cash assets on hand across many businesses or financial institutions simultaneously. In a liquidity crisis, liquidity problems at individual institutions lead to an acute increase in demand and decrease in supply of liquidity, and the resulting lack of available liquidity can lead to widespread defaults and even bankruptcies.

Understanding a Liquidity Crisis
Maturity mismatching, between assets and liabilities, as well as a resulting lack of properly timed cash flow, are typically at the root of a liquidity crisis. Liquidity problems can occur at a single institution, but a true liquidity crisis usually refers to a simultaneous lack of liquidity across many institutions or an entire financial system.

Single Business Liquidity Problem

When an otherwise solvent business does not have the liquid assets—in cash or other highly marketable assets—

necessary to meet its short-term obligations it faces a liquidity problem. Obligations can include repaying loans, paying its ongoing operational bills, and paying its employees. These business may have enough value in total assets to meet all these in the long-run, but if it does not have enough cash to pay them as they come due, then it will default and could eventually enter bankruptcy as creditors demand repayment. The root of the problem is usually a mismatch between the maturities of investments the business has made and the liabilities the business has incurred in order to finance its investments.

This produces a cash flow problem, where the anticipated revenue from the business' various projects does not arrive soon enough or in sufficient volume to make payments toward the corresponding financing. For businesses, this type of cash flow problem can be entirely avoided by the business choosing investment projects whose expected revenue matches the repayment plans for any related financing well enough to avoid any missed payments.

Alternatively, the business can try to match maturities on an ongoing basis by taking on additional short-term debt from lenders or maintaining a sufficient self-financed reserve of liquid assets on hand (in effect relying on equity holders) to make payments as they come due. Many businesses do this by relying on short-term loans to meet business needs. Often this financing is structured for less than a year and can help a company meet payroll and other demands. If a business investments and debt are mismatched in maturity, additional short-term financing is not available, and self-financed reserves are not sufficient, then the business will either need to sell other assets to generate cash, known as liquidating assets, or face default. When the company faces a shortage of liquidity, and if the liquidity problem cannot not solved by liquidating sufficient assets to meet its obligations, the company must declare bankruptcy.

Banks and financial institutions are particularly vulnerable to these kind of liquidity problems because much of their revenue is generated by lending long-term on loans for home mortgages or capital investments and borrowing short-term from depositors accounts. Maturity mismatching is a normal and inherent part of the business model of most financial institutions, and so they are usually in a continual position of needing to secure funds to meet immediate obligations, either through additional short-term debt, self-financed reserves, or liquidating long-term assets.

Liquidity Crisis
Individual financial institutions are not the only ones who can have a liquidity problem. When many financial institutions experience a simultaneous shortage of liquidity and draw down their self-financed reserves, seek additional short-term debt from credit markets, or try to sell-off assets to generate cash, a liquidity crisis can occur. Interest rates rise, minimum required reserve limits become a binding constraint, and assets fall in value or become unsaleable as everyone tries to sell at once. The acute need for liquidity across institutions becomes a mutually self-reinforcing positive feedback loop that can spread to impact institutions and businesses that were not initially facing any liquidity problem on their own.

Entire countries—and their economies—can become engulfed in this situation. For the economy as a whole, a liquidity crisis means that the two main sources of liquidity in the economy—banks loans and the commercial paper market—become suddenly scarce. Banks reduce the number of loans they make or stop making loans altogether. Because so many non-financial companies rely on these loans to meet their short-term obligations, this lack of lending has a ripple effect throughout the economy. In a trickle-down effect, the lack of funds impacts a plethora of companies, which in turn affects individuals employed by those firms.A liquidity crisis can unfold in in response to a specific economic shock or as a feature of a normal business cycle. For example, during the financial crisis of the Great Recession, many banks and non-bank institutions had significant portions of their cash come from short-term funds that were put towards financing long-term mortgages. When short-term interest rates rose and real estate prices collapsed, such arrangements forced a liquidity crisis.

A negative shock to economic expectations might drive the deposit holders with a bank or banks to make sudden, large withdrawals, if not their entire accounts. This may be due to concerns about the stability of the specific institution or broader economic influences. The account holder may see a need to have cash in hand immediately, perhaps if widespread economic declines are feared. Such activity can leave banks deficient in cash and unable to cover all registered accounts.

BEST AND FINAL OFFER: DEFINITION, STRATEGIES FOR BUYERS & SELLERS

A best and final offer in real estate is a prospective buyer's last and highest offer for a property. The best and final offer is typically submitted in response to a bidding war. A seller who has received several offers will ask all bidders or the top bidders to submit their best and final offers rather than trying to negotiate individually with each bidder. The term is also used in government contracting. An agency will ask bidders to submit their last and final offers to ensure all parties have the ability to submit their most competitive pricing for a job.

How a Best and Final Offer Works

The best and final offer in a real estate bid is the most favorable terms the buyer is willing to offer the seller for the purchase of the property. A seller who receives multiple offers will resolve the situation by asking each bidder to submit only one offer that represents their best and final offer. This process is often not undertaken unless it is merited; if a seller has received a competitive offer for their house or did not receive many bids, a best and final offer process is not warranted. The process often starts with the elimination of non-competitive prospective buyers. However, the seller may decide to open this process up to other buyers, even ones that previously did not submit an original bud. The seller's agent notifies all parties involved of a deadline to submit one final offer shortly. This deadline is often no longer than several days.

Each best and final offer isn't limited to just price. Buyers should be prepared to submit lender pre-approval documentation, a clear financial profile, a personal biography, and non-financial terms including inspection and closing preferences. Best and final offers may also still be submitted as a price range to demonstrate the buyer's preferred price and maximum price, though the seller may stipulate specific pricing to avoid continual negotiations.

Motives for Best and Final Offers

In real estate, there's several reasons a seller may initiate a best and final offer:

The seller wants to sell faster. Instead of having to navigate multiple rounds of negotiations, the seller may only be interested in working with the most interested party. By kicking off a best and final offer process, the seller is signaling to prospective buyers that they want to skip past some of the early-stage discussions and move directly toward late-stage negotiations.

The seller received too many offers. There may have been tremendous interest in the seller's property, and they simply can't decide how to otherwise narrow down the offers. Some may have the most favorable price, while others may have more favorable terms or flexibility. If the seller feels there are more than enough parties to warrant a best and final offer, it will use this technique to weed out non-competitive offers and only move forward with the most interested parties.

The seller wants the best price. This technique doesn't always work, but a best and final offer is a signal to prospective buyers to make their offer as appealing as possible. This includes escalation clauses or waiving inspections. While a best and final offer may scare away potential buyers, it also has the potential to incite a bidding war between the top parties.

In the government sector, government entities are frequently mandated to choose vendors and suppliers who offer the lowest possible prices for the requested services and products. The manager of the procurement process is still permitted to weigh other factors such as the reliability and competence of the vendor in addition to the final offer price. Most often, there are strict bidding processes that stipulate what these agencies must ask of suppliers, including one final and best offer. A call for best and final offers is also a signal to the real estate market that you are intent on selling your home. While other deals may have prolonged timelines, a signal for participants to submit top offers indicates a short timeline to make a deal happen.

Special Considerations

The buyer who gave the winning best and final offer may also withdraw the bid. This may be because of new information that became available about the property or questions about the bidding process including whether or not there actually were other bidders driving up the price. As with any offer that is dependent on the outcome of contingencies, acceptance of a best and final offer bid does not guarantee a deal will close..Most often, a best and final offer is communicated as non-negotiable by the seller. It is expected that all offers are as-is, and the seller must decide to either accept or reject (not negotiate) all offers.

Consideration for Real Estate Buyers

If a property is expected to be competitive, buyers may consider distancing them from all other parties with a very strong initial bid. Instead of leaving the door open to other buyers, the seller may take note of the serious offer and decide to only negotiate directly with the top bidder..Real estate agents and brokers play a key part in crafting best and final offers. If it comes time to prepare one last bid, buyers often rely on their broker's experience to guide them on the specifications, layout, and intricacies that make their offer stand out. If you're in a situation where you're asked to submit a best and final offer, attempt to find out what the seller wants through your agent. There may be specific conditions the seller is most interested in, and you're at an advantage if you're able to obtain this information prior to submitting your offer.

Consideration for Real Estate Sellers

A critical part of the best and final offer process is determining whether one is needed. A best and final offer process may scare away interested parties, especially if market conditions have softened. Buyers may drop out of the bidding process, withdrawing their previously strong offers.

It's often not recommended to move forward with a best and final offer process unless there are at least three strong bids.

Prior to kicking off a best and final offer process, leverage your agent's experience to provide an unbiased evaluation of offers and whether you are receiving fair value. While it's understanding to want to maximize the return on your home, buyers that have already submit fair offers may turn elsewhere if they do not feel your requested terms are favorable to all parties.

When evaluating final offers, consider the buyer's profile and their ability to close at the agreed price. Their price may be most enticing; however, review relevant lending documents and tax returns to understand their personal finances to minimize the risk of them not securing financing.

Consideration for Government Entities

For government agencies entertaining requests for proposals, an interesting conflict arises when evaluating diversity and inclusion initiatives. A company may submit the lowest price with the most favorable conditions. However, more entities are striving to obtain inclusivity targets. Each government entity should have guidance on how to evaluate bids and select between favorable terms and target demographic. Government agencies often send a letter often citing that negotiations have concluded for the request, That letter outlines the opportunity to submit one final packet, the cutoff date for submission, and provisions of the submission such as the method and information to be submitted.

Best and final offer bids are often required to be in writing and signed by an authorized representative or executive of the vendor or supplier. If a best and final offer is made verbally to expedite negotiations, the offer must often be certified and confirmed in writing afterward. Some entities have conditions or guidance on reopening discussions after best and final offers have been submitted. In some situations where a government agency wants to further discuss terms with one specific offeror, the agency may be required to reopen the potential for discussion with all offerors.

What Is a Best and Final Offer?

A best and final offer is a call to interested parties to submit the most ideal contract conditions. It is often the final round of discussion during the sale of a property; once the best and final offers are in, the seller often selects the best one and works directly with the buyer with the most favorable terms. A best and final offer is also prevalent in government agencies that seek proposals for jobs. After an initial round of bids, government agencies may ask the companies with the best offers to submit one final bid with the lowest price they are willing to contract for.

A seller is not obligated to accept any offer they do not feel is fair, including best and final offers. Like all other offers for real estate property, a best and final offer is binding once a contract has been signed. However, the agreement may still fall apart if the buyer fails to obtain financing or if contingencies are not met. In addition, a buyer or seller may back out at any time, though they may be required to pay penalties, fees, or lose earnest deposits. The seller can reopen negotiations after best and final offers have been selected. Most often, the seller will select the most interesting offer and negotiate directly with only the top bidder. However, the goal of a best and final offer is to have a package that does not need to be negotiated (or requires very little negotiation).

How Do You Win a Best and Final Offer?

Every seller is different, so it's to your advantage to understand what is most important to the other party. Use your real estate to get information on what the seller is most interested in. Then, craft your final offer to cater most to what they are looking for. For example, a seller interested in a quick sale may accept a lower offer if you waive all inspections and reduce contingencies.

HAGGLE: WHAT IT MEANS, HOW IT WORKS, CONSIDERATIONS

To haggle is when two parties involved in a transaction such as the purchase of a good and service negotiate the price until both parties can mutually agree on a fair price. The process of haggling involves two parties making sequential offers and counteroffers to each other until a price is agreed upon. The individual trying to buy the good and service is trying to pay the least amount possible, while the seller's primary objective is to maximize the selling price. Haggling also may go by the names bargaining, quibbling, dickering, or informal negotiating. The act of haggling has been around since ancient times and continues to this day. It is a common practice in real estate negotiations, car purchases, and at informal flea markets— while it is rarely used in retail settings such as at supermarkets, pharmacies, or brand-name clothing stores. Haggling is a technique that involves two or more parties making sequential offers and counteroffers until an agreement is made.

Understanding Haggle

Not all transactions are open to bargaining. Both religious beliefs and regional customs may determine whether or not the seller is willing to engage in bargaining. Globally, haggling has different accepted levels of tolerance. In Europe and North America, haggling is generally accepted for larger ticket items like automobiles, jewelry, and real estate—but not for smaller day-to-day items like combs or a gallon of milk. However, in other regions around the world, haggling for smaller items is generally accepted and is part of the culture. In these regions, children are taught to haggle at a young age to ensure that they are receiving the best-perceived deal when making any type of purchase. The acceptance of haggling can also be determined by location. In department and grocery stores, haggling is often expressly prohibited, but at places like flea markets, outdoor marketplaces, and bazaars, haggling is accepted and encouraged. Many consider haggling to be an art and a skill of persuasion rather than a rational economic activity. To haggle is the same as to bargain or to informally negotiate.

Special Considerations
Various economic theories have been proposed to explain the process of haggling. The behavioral theory proposes that certain people have different personalities or dispositions toward negotiations rather than taking prices as they are given. The game theory proposes solutions to bargaining problems as part of strategic action and can be interpreted as part of reaching a Nash Equilibrium. Haggling is also considered when considering retail pricing theory. Mainstream (neoclassical) economics, however, supposes that all market prices are jointly determined by supply and demand and so there would be no need for haggling since all prices would always reflect an equilibrium level.

5 NEGOTIATING STRATEGIES WHEN SELLING YOUR HOME

Selling your home is likely one of the biggest financial transactions you'll undertake in your lifetime, and the price you agree on with a buyer, along with the real estate commissions you pay, will determine how much money you walk away with. These negotiating strategies could put you in the driver's seat and help you get top dollar in any market.

1. Counter at Your List Price

As a seller, you probably won't want to accept a potential buyer's initial bid on your home if it's below your asking price. Buyers usually expect a back-and-forth negotiation, so their initial offer will often be lower than your list price—but it may also be lower than what they're actually willing to pay. At this point most sellers will make a counteroffer with a price that's higher but still below their list price, because they're afraid of losing the potential sale.

They want to seem flexible and willing to negotiate to close the deal. This strategy does indeed work in terms of getting the property sold, as thousands of sellers can attest, but it's not necessarily the best way to get top dollar.

Instead of dropping your price, counter by sticking to your listed purchase price. Someone who really wants to buy will remain engaged and come back to you with a higher offer. Assuming that you've priced your property fairly to begin with, countering at your list price says that you know what your property is worth and you intend to get the money you deserve. Buyers may be surprised, and some will be turned off by your unwillingness to negotiate. You do risk having a buyer walk away when you use this strategy. However, you'll also avoid wasting time on buyers who make lowball offers and won't close any deal unless they can get a bargain. A variation on countering at your list price is to counter just slightly below it, conceding by perhaps $1,000. Use this approach when you want to be tough but are afraid that appearing too inflexible will drive away buyers.

2. Reject the Offer

If you're gutsy enough, you can try a negotiation tactic that's more extreme than countering at your list price: Reject the buyer's offer—but don't counter at all. To keep them in the game, you then ask them to submit a new offer. If they're really interested, and you haven't turned them off, they will.

This strategy sends a stronger signal that you know your property is worth what you're asking for it. If the buyer resubmits, they'll have to make a higher offer—unless they decide to play hardball back and submit the same or even a lower offer. When you don't counter, you're not ethically locked into a negotiation with a particular buyer, and you can accept a higher offer if it comes along. For the buyer, knowing that someone may make a better offer at any moment creates pressure to submit a more competitive offer quickly if they really want the property. This strategy can be particularly useful if the property has only been on the market for a short time or if you have an open house coming up.

3. Try to Create a Bidding War

Speaking of open houses: Make them an integral part of your process. After listing the home on the market and making it available to be shown, schedule an open house for a few days later. Refuse to entertain any offers until after the open house. Potential buyers will expect to be in competition and may place higher offers as a result. If you get multiple offers, you can go back to the top bidders and ask for their highest and best offers. Of course, the open house may yield only one offer, but the party offering it won't know that, so you'll have a psychological edge going forward with counteroffers, etc.

While it is possible to field multiple offers on a home from several buyers simultaneously, it is considered unethical to accept a better offer from a new buyer while in negotiations with any other buyer.

4. Put an Expiration Date on Your Counteroffer

Say a buyer submits an offer that you don't want to accept, and you counter their offer. You're then involved in a negotiation with that party, and generally it is considered unethical to accept a better offer from another buyer if one comes along, though it is not illegal. It is possible, as noted above, to be involved in multiple negotiations with several buyers at the same time. It is the seller's prerogative to disclose or not disclose this information to the prospective buyers. Disclosure can result in higher offers, but it can also frighten off a buyer. The seller is legally allowed to counter more than one offer at the same time, but they must include appropriate language letting all the parties know of the situation.

In the interest of selling your home quickly, consider putting an expiration date on your counteroffers. This strategy compels the buyer to make a decision, so you can either get your home under contract or move on. Don't make the deadline so short that the buyer is turned off, but consider making it shorter than the default time frame in your state's standard real estate contract. If the default expiration is three days, you might shorten it to one or two days. In addition to closing the deal quickly, there's another reason to push sellers to make a fast decision. While the counteroffer is outstanding, your home is effectively off the market. Many buyers won't submit an offer when another negotiation is underway. And if the deal falls through, you've added time to the official number of days your home has been on the market. The more days your home is on the market, the less desirable it appears, and the more likely you are to have to lower your asking price to get a buyer.

5. Agree to Pay Closing Costs

It seems like it's become standard practice for buyers to ask the seller to pay their closing costs. These costs can amount to about 3% of the purchase price and cover what seem to be a lot of frivolous fees. Buyers are often feeling cash-strapped from the down payment, moving expenses, the prospect of redecorating costs—and maybe even from paying the closing costs on the home they sold. Some buyers can't afford to close the deal at all without assistance for closing costs. While many buyers don't have or don't want to spend extra cash up front to get into the home, they can often afford to borrow a little bit more. If you give them the cash they want for closing costs, the transaction may be more likely to proceed.

When a buyer submits an offer and asks you to pay the closing costs, counter with your willingness to pay but at an increased purchase price, even if it means going above your list price. Buyers sometimes don't realize that when they ask the seller to pay their closing costs, they're effectively lowering the home's sale price. As the seller, of course, you'll see the bottom line very clearly. You can increase your asking price by enough to still get as high as your list price after paying the buyer's closing costs. If your list price is $200,000, and the buyer offers $190,000 with $6,000 toward closing, you would counter with something between $196,000 and $206,000, with $6,000 for closing costs. A catch is that the price plus closing costs must be supported when the home is appraised; otherwise, you'll have to lower it later to close the deal, because the buyer's lender won't approve an overpriced sale.

The key to executing these negotiating strategies successfully is that you have to be offering a superior product. The home needs to show well, be in excellent condition, and have something that competing properties do not if you want to have the upper hand in negotiations. If buyers aren't excited about the property you're offering, your hardball tactics won't cause them to up their game. They'll just walk away.

The Art of Negotiating With Impact

Negotiating is the art of getting past the word 'NO'. A skilled negotiator has the ability to persuade. However, it is also important to adopt a respectful, ethical, collaborative approach in an effort to come to an agreement. .Negotiating, put simply, is two parties with competing needs working towards an agreement on how they will cooperate (Tillet, 1991). Its basic components include:

Preparation

Objectivity

Strategy

Technique

Even the most skilled negotiator had to start with the basics. So, what do you need to learn to get started? First, you need to learn how to prepare for negotiation if you want to succeed. Then focus on objectivity. Learn how to assess your strengths, weaknesses and goals. By assessing your weak points versus your strengths, objectively, you will be better equipped to reach your negotiation goals. The final step involves developing a strategy based on a realistic course of action combined with techniques harnessed to conclude a win-win negotiation.

Top Tip: As part of your technique, stay pleasant and listen. This will allow you to remain calm and think clearly. Especially if someone is reacting negatively in any way. By listening you will give yourself time to evaluate the situation and respond accordingly.

Do I really need to research?

In preparation for your meeting, it is vital that you get data – information is power! Including facts and statistics in your negotiation can establish credibility and make a significant impact. You should also have alternatives prepared while remaining clear about what is important to you.

Top Tip: If their offer is unbelievably good, blandly acknowledge and restate the offer.

CONCLUSION

Negotiating is essential part of day-to-life, the business world, and international affairs. Regardless of what you're negotiating, being a successful negotiator means knowing what you want, trying to understand the other party's (or parties') position, and compromising if necessary. A successful negotiation leaves everyone satisfied that they have gotten a deal they can live with.

Negotiation is the means by which people deal with their differences. Therefore, some people experience a fear of conflict and failure. To negotiate is to reach a mutual agreement. The key here is to remain objective. Don't take anything said personally. Be prepared, be ready to listen, be a thoughtful objective observer – ready to navigate the process with the strategies and techniques you have acquired. The importance of being a good negotiator cannot be disputed. Negotiating is an intrinsic part of everyday life. We negotiate daily, from when we wake to when we sleep, with friends, family, and colleagues for a wide variety of things. Becoming a skilled negotiator can reduce the amount of stress we experience regularly and significantly improve our chances of success.